States

MISSISSIPPI

by Jordan Mills

CAPSTONE PRESS
a capstone imprint

Next Page Books are published by Capstone Press,
1710 Roe Crest Drive, North Mankato, Minnesota 56003
www.mycapstone.com

Library of Congress Cataloging-in-Publication Data
Cataloging-in-publication information is on file with the Library of
Congress.
ISBN 978-1-5157-0411-9 (library binding)
ISBN 978-1-5157-0470-6 (paperback)
ISBN 978-1-5157-0522-2 (ebook PDF)

Editorial Credits
Jaclyn Jaycox, editor; Richard Korab and Katy LaVigne, designers;
Morgan Walters, media researcher; Laura Manthe, production specialist

Photo Credits
Alamy: North Wind Picture Archives, 26, PARIS PIERCE, 27; Capstone
Press: Angi Gahler, map 4, 7; Corbis: CORBIS, 12; Dreamstime:
Blewis49, 14, Marcio Silva, top left 21; Getty Images: Hulton Archive,
middle 18; Glow Images: Superstock, 25; Library of Congress: Prints
and Photographs Division/New York World Telegram and the Sun
Newspaper Photograph Collection/Orlando Fernandez, middle 19;
Newscom: Album/Prisma, 9, Jeremy Woodhouse Blend Images, 5,
PHOTOlink, bottom 18; One Mile Up, Inc., flag, seal 23; Shutterstock:
Allen Berezovsky, top 19, Antoly Vlasov, top right 21, Beth Swanson,
bottom right 20, Daniel Prudek, bottom left 21, Dave McDearmont, 15,
DFree, top 18, eZeePics Studio, middle left 21, Featureflash, bottom
19, Fotoluminate LLC, 7, inigocia, 16, JayL, bottom right 8, jennyt,
top right 20, Jill Nightingale, bottom left 20, John Brueske, 6, Joseph
Sohm, 11, Juan G. Aunion, bottom right 21, kaband, middle right 21,
Marcin Pawinski, bottom 24, michaeljung, top 24, Nagel Photography,
13, R_Szatkowski, top left 20, Rob Hainer, bottom left 8, Robert A.
Mansker, 29, Virunja, cover; Wikimedia: NatalieMaynor, 10, 17, US
Government, 28

All design elements by Shutterstock

Printed and bound in China.
0316/CA21600187
012016   009436F16

TABLE OF CONTENTS

Want to take your research further? Ask your librarian if your school subscribes to PebbleGo Next. If so, when you see this helpful symbol 🖱 throughout the book, log onto www.pebblegonext.com for bonus downloads and information.

LOCATION

Mississippi is one of America's southern states. It's in a region often called the Deep South. To the north of Mississippi is Tennessee. Alabama lies along Mississippi's eastern edge. The mighty Mississippi River forms most of Mississippi's western border. Arkansas and Louisiana are on the west. Louisiana also borders part of southern Mississippi. The rest of the southern border faces the Gulf of Mexico. A string of islands off the coast is also part of Mississippi. Jackson, the state capital, is the largest city. Next in size are Gulfport, Southhaven, and Hattiesburg.

PebbleGo Next Bonus!
To print and label your own map, go to www.pebblegonext.com and search keywords:

MS MAP

4

The city of Jackson is named after Andrew Jackson. He was a military hero and America's seventh president.

GEOGRAPHY

Mississippi has rivers, flat plains, and rolling hills. Many rivers in eastern Mississippi empty into the Gulf of Mexico. Several rivers in the state's western and northern areas feed into the Mississippi River. The Mississippi Floodplain is a narrow strip of land in southwestern Mississippi. It runs along the east side of the Mississippi River. The Eastern Gulf Coastal Plain covers the rest of the state. Lowlands, prairies, forests, and hills cover most of this region. Woodall Mountain is the state's highest point. It is 806 feet (246 meters) above sea level.

PebbleGo Next Bonus! To watch a video about Natchez, go to www.pebblegonext.com and search keywords:

MS VIDEO

The Mississippi River is about 2,320 miles (3,730 kilometers) long.

The Mississippi River ends at the Gulf of Mexico on the southern border of the state.

Legend

▲ Highest Point
⬭ Lake
∿ River

Pickwick Lake
▲ Woodall Mountain
Sardis Lake
Grenada Lake
Mississippi River
DELTA
Tombigbee River
Yazoo River
Big Black River
EASTERN GULF COASTAL PLAIN
Ross Barnett Reservoir
Okatibbee Reservoir
Pearl River
MISSISSIPPI FLOODPLAIN
Pascagoula River

Scale
Miles
0 20 40 60 80
0 20 40 60 80
Kilometers

Gulf of Mexico

WEATHER

Mississippi has mild winters and hot summers. The average January temperature is 46 degrees Fahrenheit (8 degrees Celsius). The average July temperature is 81°F (27°C).

Average High and Low Temperatures (Jackson, MS)

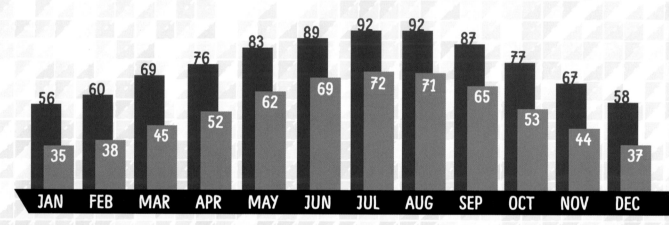

	JAN	FEB	MAR	APR	MAY	JUN	JUL	AUG	SEP	OCT	NOV	DEC
High	56	60	69	76	83	89	92	92	87	77	67	58
Low	35	38	45	52	62	69	72	71	65	53	44	37

Old Capitol Museum of Mississippi History

In Jackson visitors can explore the Old Capitol, which was built in the 1830s. It served as the state's capitol building from 1839 to 1903. It now houses the Old Capitol Museum of Mississippi History, which details American Indian and pioneer life, the Civil War, and the roles of the government.

Vicksburg National Cemetery

The Vicksburg National Cemetery is the largest Civil War cemetery in the country. The 116-acre (47-hectare) cemetery is the final resting place for 17,000 Union soldiers.

Stennis Space Center

The Stennis Space Center in Hancock County is the nation's largest rocket test station. At the visitor center, people can view real rocket engines and go inside a model of the *International Space Station*.

HISTORY AND GOVERNMENT

Union forces drove back Confederate troops at Champion Hill, Mississippi, during the Civil War.

Mississippi was once home to thousands of American Indians, including the Natchez, Choctaw, and Chickasaw Indians. Hernando de Soto of Spain explored the area from 1540 to 1541. In 1682 French explorer René-Robert Cavelier, known as Sieur de La Salle, claimed the Mississippi Valley, including Mississippi, for France.

Mississippi became British territory in 1763. After the Revolutionary War (1775–1783), Britain's land went to the United States. The Mississippi Territory was created in 1798. Many settlers soon moved into the area to farm. In 1817 Mississippi became the 20th state.

Mississippi's state government is divided into three branches. Mississippi's governor leads the executive branch. The legislature consists of the 52-member Senate and the 122-member House of Representatives. The judicial branch is made up of judges and their courts. They uphold the laws.

The state capitol building is located in Jackson.

INDUSTRY

Service industries make up a large part of Mississippi's economy. Service workers include people in sales, real estate, banking, and health care. Tourism is an important service industry in Mississippi. The state has many attractions, including hunting, fishing, riverboat casinos, national parks, and historic mansions.

Manufacturing is a major industry in the state. Mississippians make many products from the state's natural resources, including petroleum, natural gas, clay, and wood products. Mississippi is also known as one of the top shipbuilding states.

Visitors can take a cruise on a steamboat and explore the Mississippi River.

Agriculture employs about 29 percent of Mississippi's workforce. Cotton and soybeans are major crops. Livestock and other animal products are a large part of the state's agriculture. Mississippi's location on the Gulf of Mexico hclps makc it a major producer of seafood.

The commercial shrimp industry has been an important part of Mississippi's econonmy.

POPULATION

White people are Mississippi's largest ethnic group. More than 1.7 million white people live in the state. Most white Mississippians have roots in Ireland, Scotland, England, France, Germany, and other European countries.

About 1 million African-Americans live in Mississippi. African-Americans make up nearly 37 percent of the state population. This is the highest percentage of African-Americans of any state.

Population by Ethnicity

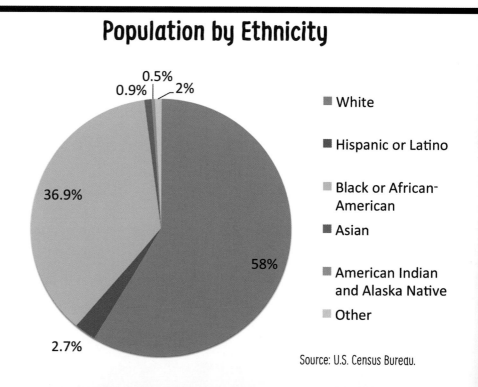

- White
- Hispanic or Latino
- Black or African-American
- Asian
- American Indian and Alaska Native
- Other

0.5%
0.9%
2%
36.9%
58%
2.7%

Source: U.S. Census Bureau.

The rest of Mississippi's population comes from many backgrounds. These include Hispanics and people of varied Asian descent. A little more than 80,000 Hispanics live in the state, while about 25,000 Asians call Mississippi home. A small number of American Indians also live in Mississippi.

FAMOUS PEOPLE

Oprah Winfrey (1954–) was the host of the popular *Oprah Winfrey Show* for 25 seasons. She received an Academy Award nomination for her role in the movie *The Color Purple* (1985). She now leads her own TV channel. She was born in Kosciusko.

Medgar Evers (1925–1963) was a civil rights leader. He fought for voting rights and school integration. He was born in Decatur. He was shot and killed near his home in Jackson.

Jim Henson (1936–1990) was a puppeteer. He invented Miss Piggy, Kermit the Frog, and the other Muppets. He was born in Greenville.

Brett Favre (1969–) was a star quarterback in the National Football League (NFL). He played most of his career with the Green Bay Packers. Favre is now retired. He was born in Gulfport.

Tennessee Williams (1911–1983) wrote plays. He won Pulitzer Prizes for *A Streetcar Named Desire* (1947) and *Cat on a Hot Tin Roof* (1955). He was born in Columbus.

Britney Spears (1981–) is a singer and entertainer. Her hit songs include "Oops!... I Did It Again" and "Baby One More Time." She was born in McComb.

STATE SYMBOLS

magnolia

magnolia

mockingbird

largemouth bass

PebbleGo Next Bonus! To make a dessert the color of Mississippi soil, go to www.pebblegonext.com and search keywords:

MS RECIPE

Fossil

prehistoric whale

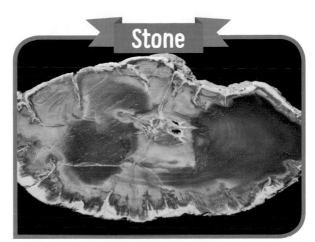

Stone

petrified wood

Water Mammal

bottlenose dolphin

Shell

oyster shell

Insect

honeybee

Waterfowl

wood duck

FAST FACTS

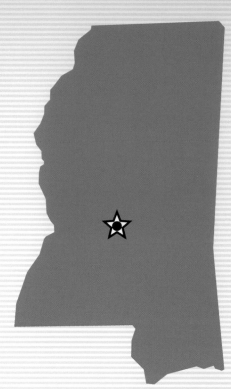

STATEHOOD

1817

CAPITAL ☆

Jackson

LARGEST CITY •

Jackson

SIZE

46,923 square miles (121,530 square kilometers) land area (2010 U.S. Census Bureau)

POPULATION

2,991,207 (2013 U.S. Census estimate)

STATE NICKNAME

Magnolia State

STATE MOTTO

"Virtute et Armis," which is Latin for "By Valor and Arms"

STATE SEAL

Mississippi adopted its official state seal in 1894. The seal shows an eagle with widespread wings. On the eagle's breast is a shield with stars and stripes. The eagle holds an olive branch in its right talon and three arrows in its left. The olive branch stands for the desire for peace. The arrows represent war. Below the eagle is a single star. The words "The Great Seal of the State of Mississippi" are in a circle around the border.

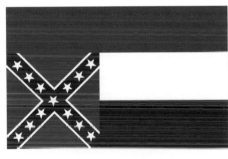

PebbleGo Next Bonus! To print and color your own flag, go to www.pebblegonext.com and search keywords:

MS FLAG

STATE FLAG

The state legislature adopted Mississippi's flag in 1894. The flag has three horizontal stripes. The stripes are red, white, and blue, which are the national colors. A Confederate flag is in the upper left corner. Mississippi was a Confederate state in the Civil War. The Confederate flag has a blue "X" outlined in white on a red background. The 13 white stars on the X stand for the original 13 colonies.

MINING PRODUCTS

petroleum, natural gas, coal, sand and gravel

MANUFACTURED GOODS

petroleum and coal, chemicals, food products, machinery, furniture, plastics and rubber products

FARM PRODUCTS

chickens, wood, cotton, catfish, soybeans, rice, wheat

PebbleGo Next Bonus!
To learn the lyrics to
the state song, go to
www.pebblegonext.com
and search keywords:

MS SONG

MISSISSIPPI TIMELINE

1500

Chickasaw, Choctaw, and Natchez Indians live in the area that is now Mississippi.

1540

Spanish explorer Hernando de Soto reaches Mississippi while searching for gold.

1620

The Pilgrims establish a colony in the New World in present-day Massachusetts.

1682

French explorer René-Robert Cavelier, known as Sieur de La Salle, claims the Mississippi Valley, including Mississippi, for France.

1699

Frenchman Pierre Le Moyne starts the first settlement in the Mississippi area at Fort Maurepas.

 **1763** Mississippi becomes British territory.

 **1775–1783** American colonists fight for their independence from Great Britain in the Revolutionary War.

 **1783** Mississippi becomes U.S. territory, except for the Gulf Coast area.

1798 The Mississippi Territory is created.

 1817 Mississippi becomes the 20th state on December 10.

1861 Mississippi becomes the second of 11 states to leave the Union and join the Confederate States of America.

1861–1865 The Union and the Confederacy fight the Civil War. Almost half of Mississippi's 78,000 soldiers die during the war.

1907 Boll weevils destroy much of Mississippi's cotton crop.

1914–1918 World War I is fought; the United States enters the war in 1917.

1939–1945 World War II is fought; the United States enters the war in 1941.

1962 James Meredith enrolls as the first African-American student at the University of Mississippi.

1979 The Pearl River floods, devastating Jackson and other cities along the river.

1991 Kirk Fordice becomes the first Republican to be elected governor of Mississippi since 1874.

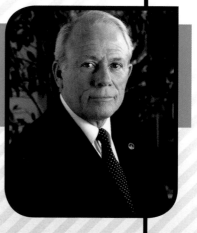

2005

Hurricane Katrina makes landfall near the Louisiana-Mississippi border on August 29. The storm kills about 1,800 people, leaves hundreds of thousands of people homeless, and causes about $100 billion in damage. It is one of the most destructive storms to ever strike the United States.

2010

An explosion on an offshore oil rig kills 11 people and causes millions of gallons of oil to pour into the Gulf of Mexico. Oil from the spill reaches the Mississippi coast, harming the state's fishing and tourism industries.

2015

The Mississippi State University rocketry team takes the championship at the 2015 Intercollegiate Rocket Engineering Competition; the team's rocket reached a top speed of Mach 1.51, or about 1,150 miles (1,851 kilometers) per hour.

Glossary

casino *(kuh-SEE-noh)*—a place where adults gamble

descend *(dee-SEND)*—if you are descended from someone, you belong to a later generation of the same family

ethnic *(ETH-nik)*—related to a group of people and their culture

executive *(ig-ZE-kyuh-tiv)*—the branch of government that makes sure laws are followed

industry *(IN-duh-stree)*—a business which produces a product or provides a service

integration *(in-ti-GRAY-shuhn)*—the act or practice of making facilities or an organization open to people of all races

judicial *(joo-DISH-uhl)*—to do with the branch of government that explains and interprets the laws

legislature *(LEJ-iss-lay-chur)*—a group of elected officials who have the power to make or change laws for a country or state

mansion *(MAN-shuhn)*—a very large and impressive house

petroleum *(puh-TROH-lee-uhm)*—an oily liquid found below the earth's surface used to make gasoline, heating oil, and many other products

tourism *(TOOR-i-zuhm)*—the business of taking care of visitors to a country or place

Read More

Gaines, Ann. *Mississippi.* It's My State! New York: Cavendish Square Publishing, 2014.

Ganeri, Anita. *United States of America: A Benjamin Blog and His Inquisitive Dog Guide.* Country Guides. Chicago: Heinemann Raintree, 2015.

Yasuda, Anita. *What's Great About Mississippi?* Our Great States. Minneapolis: Lerner Publications, 2015.

Internet Sites

FactHound offers a safe, fun way to find Internet sites related to this book. All of the sites on FactHound have been researched by our staff.

Here's all you do:

Visit *www.facthound.com*

Type in this code: 9781515704119

Check out projects, games and lots more at
www.capstonekids.com

Critical Thinking Using the Common Core

1. Tourism is an important service industry in Mississippi. What attractions does the state have? (Key Ideas and Details)

2. According to the pie chart on page 16, what two ethnic groups make up the majority of Mississippi's population? (Integration of Knowledge and Ideas)

3. What resulted from the 2010 explosion of an offshore oil rig? (Key Ideas and Details)

Index